The Little Book Of Secrets

12 Essential Ideas To Give Your Life The Boost It Needs

This book may be purchased for educational, business or sales promotional use. For information, please write Special Promotions, 1683 Langley, Irvine, CA 92614

Printed in the United States of America

Library of Congress Cataloging-in-Publication Data

Gunhus, Jeff

A Little Book Of Secrets / Jeff Gunhus

ISBN 1-4486-8137-5

For Nicole, Jackson, William, Daniel and Caroline

Table of Secrets

INTRODUCTION

KNOWLEDGE IS NOT POWER

What counts is not the size of the dog in the fight, but the size of the fight in the dog.

-Dwight D. Eisenhower

I want to share some secrets with you, but I've got to get something off my chest first.

Reading this book may be a waste of time.

Let me explain.

Without reading a single page of this book, you probably know something you could do right now to improve your life.

Am I right?

There are actions you could take today to accomplish something you have been meaning to do for a long time.

Whether it is to finally send your resume to a company you want to work for, join a gym to get into shape, go back to school to get that advanced degree, or simply tell a loved one how much you appreciate their support and love, you know there are things you could do right now to make a change in your life.

You know the things you should or could do to make a positive impact on the world around you. Volunteer at a charity, be active in your church, mentor an inner city kid.

But knowing is never enough.

There is no power in knowledge.

True power is found only in action.

We are about to embark on a journey together. I just want to make sure we know where we're going.

In the following pages, I am going to share with you the essential techniques, methods and mental attitudes I believe are necessary for someone to live a fulfilled life of peak performance grounded in strong values.

I know with certainty these secrets work.

I have used them in my own career as my partners and I built a $40 million organization with over 2000 employees. I have taught them to hundreds of others who point to them as essential factors in their own success stories.

And, I should advise you, these are not new ideas. Early in my life I thrust myself into the success literature to figure out what made accomplished people tick. I read everything from Dale Carnegie to Anthony Robbins. I interviewed successful people to draw my own conclusions and to help separate the solid advice from the motivational rah-rah that flowed thick in many of those books and tapes.

The 12 Secrets I'm about to share represent what I feel is the essential distillation of all these books and speakers coupled with my own experience as an entrepreneur, a husband and a father of four.

And I'm terrified it's going to be a monumental waste of your time.

Knowledge is not power. We've already established that. So I have a problem.

My purpose here is to make you a more powerful force in your own life...and knowledge is the only weapon I've got.

These next pages will teach you what you need to know to have the success you crave.

The execution of the ideas will be entirely up to you.

Since you're already avoiding the actions you know you could execute right now that would dramatically improve your life, what chance do I have of making an impact on you?

What good will it do to just give you a longer list of things you're not going to do?

Not much.

Action is the currency of the successful and they spend it like fiends.

Not a day goes by that a successful person doesn't move themselves along from Point A toward some future goal. That's not to imply that they are workaholics. A full and deep relationship with a family member or spouse is as legitimate a goal as one focused on a career objective.

Whether this book is a worthwhile investment of your time will depend entirely on your ability to translate intention into performance.

To help you along the way, many of the secrets I share are about mindset and the worldview successful people employ to help them take action while other stand idly by.

These chapters are every bit as important as the more tangible, concrete methods taught throughout. Without the right mindset, these ideas will just stay ideas and you will not achieve your potential.

If you will commit now to putting these secrets into action, I can commit to you that you will experience significant improvements in your lifestyle, your fulfillment, and that even your most far-fetched aspirations can be brought within your reach.

Some may read this promise and roll their eyes. That's fine. Typically, the older the reader, the more the whole eye thing happens.

I get it.

Adult life can be a rough sandpaper that wears down the sharp clarity of youth.

Early visions of achievement and grandeur are pushed down and beaten back by newly accepted definitions of 'reasonable,' and 'practical.'

The fast, exciting life some imagined for themselves has instead turned out to be a mind-numbing routine broken up periodically by a week-long vacation.

The justifications for settling for less come fast and furious, too.

The 'anything is possible' mentality of youth is replaced by the 'it's just not that easy' mentality of maturity.

When we are young, it seems completely logical to quit a job you hate and take a year off to travel the world, work for world peace, live in poverty and write a book, or start a new business on a shoestring and a prayer.

As we get older, these types of options seem more and more unreasonable.

Think about that.

Subjected to reason, sudden change from a state where we are unhappy to a state where we are happy seems like a bad idea because of the risk of failure.

The pressures of society to be a 'producer' and to fit into a nice box with a job title make sudden and dramatic change wrong.

If someone quits a job or quits school to pursue a dream, they are thought of as flaky. Their friends sit back and think to themselves, "I wondered what happened to him. Guess he couldn't hack the pressure."

The old saying is that youth is wasted on the young, but I don't think so. Most older adults I know would ruin a good thing with their learned "practicality" and their "realism."

Some have accused me of having a naïve view of the world because of my faith in achievement and the limitless capacity of the human spirit.

I think the naïve ones are those who bury their heads in the sand, lost in a desert of mediocrity, and feel they have reached their capacity for greatness.

Look at the great figures of history.

Doesn't it seem impossible that a single human would be remembered by the world hundreds, even thousands of years after they died?

How could they have been so different that they stand out among the *billions* of humans that have existed?

What was so special about these people that made them different from you and me? Did they miraculously possess more than 24 hours a day?

If anything, look at the amazing advantages you have in comparison to those people.

The advances in technology, education, and health alone make your life an amazing opportunity compared to what past generations have encountered.

Knowledge is more available now than at any other point in the history of man, but still only those individuals with the courage and brashness to act will achieve greatness.

Power is from action. The power to create. The power to revolt. The power to change. The power to transform.

It all stems from action.

I'm not saying you need to fly off to the Amazon to explore the rain forest or start a political revolution, but I want to challenge you to explore the limits of your own environment.

Make a decision to act in ways that reflect your ethics and your dedication to the fulfillment of your aspirations.

Too many people accept mediocrity because they fear the actions necessary to pursue their goals and they fear failure if they try.

It's a basic human emotion rooted deep into our psyches and reinforced by the society around us. Conformity is encouraged. We are taught early on to stand in line, fill out forms, clock in when we arrive at work. It's hard to break out of that mold. I know because it's a struggle for me, too.

I'm not here to hold myself up as some guru who has life figured out. I'm in the trenches right beside you, trying to stay the course and lead a fulfilled life.

But I do feel as if my experiences and my study have equipped me with tools that make my struggle easier. These tools are what I offer today.

So, if you can put aside your fears and make the decision to put these tools into action, I can commit to you that you will experience significant improvements in your lifestyle, satisfaction and fulfillment.

If you're willing to do that, let's turn the page and get started.

SECRET #1
Create Vision, Achieve Goals

*No one ever gets very far unless he
accomplishes the impossible at
least once a day.*

-Elbert Hubbard

There is only one difference between you and
successful people:

Successful people are a success. You have the potential for success.

The distance between your potential and the
realization of your potential is determined by the
seriousness of your dedication to your goals.

What do your goals represent to you?

Are they a passing fancy?

Something that you hope to accomplish, but doubt will ever happen?

What is your level of commitment?

Every time I buy a lottery ticket my unspoken goal is to win the lottery. Otherwise, I wouldn't buy the ticket.

But it's not a real goal. It's not something I'm going to dedicate my life's work toward.

It's just fun. And if I don't achieve it (and, no, I haven't won the big bucks yet) I'm not bummed. I just shrug and move along.

Unfortunately, most people approach their life goals with the same defeatist attitude.

They have a vague idea of what they want. They plod along in what they hope is a path to get there (wherever that is.) And when they wake up one day not only off-course but on a completely different race track, they just shrug and move along.

No wonder the mid-life crisis happens.

My contention is that the best way to avoid the mid-life crisis is to work hard enough to get it right the first time.

If we solve the pre-life crisis, we can avoid the mid-life crisis…and have a hell of a lot more fun along the way.

OK. Sounds good. So how do we do it?

First, we must establish more than airy, vacuous goals that we don't really give a damn about.

We have to create a vision for where we want to go.

What is the difference between a goal and a vision?

It may just be semantics, but the word vision sings to me of the power behind an idea.

The great religions of the world were not founded by prophets who came down off the mountain, stood before their people and proclaimed, "I have a goal!"

They cried out, "I have a vision!"

A vision is a work of art. It is a product of your creative self that imagines the great possibilities of life far into the future.

It is not bound by trivial things like reality and circumstance. Vision is transcendent. Vision makes you a creator. All-powerful. Free of boundaries.

Sounds pretty good, right?

Then why do so many of us pass up this opportunity?

Why do so many of us accept the limits that society sells us?

You're too young to do that. The color of your skin is wrong. You're the wrong gender. You come from too poor a background. You're not smart enough. You're not good looking enough. You don't have enough time.

Any of those sound familiar?

So, we can do a little exercise in creating a personal vision, but that's not the new news here.

I think you have heard that part before. You've probably even done a goal setting exercise in the past.

What I want to communicate is that goals are not enough.

You must have a vision that seeps into your bones. Something that you want so badly that you can't sleep from thinking about it.

Only then will you do the hard work of the small goals necessary to achieve that vision and overcome all the doubts and setbacks that you are guaranteed to face along the way.

This vision should cover the four vital aspects of life (or you can have individual vision statements for each).

The four areas are: Career, Health, Family/Friends, Community/Faith.

Proper attention and focus on each of these vital factors will ensure you do not accomplish your vision at the detriment of a well-lived, balanced life.

Any one of these life factors is fairly easy to excel at if you focus only on that one thing. Ignore your family, your health, and participation in your church or community, and you will have more time to excel in your career.

As the old saying goes, it's not hard to make money if all you want to do is make money.

But then, on your death bed, you'll be revisiting all those wonderful hours you spent buying "stuff" instead of making a difference in the world.
By the same token, you can spend every day weeding the garden for your church, singing in the choir and opening doors for little old ladies instead of working hard to have a satisfying career. When it comes time to pay for your kid's college or pay the medical bills for an unexpected illness, you will be left unable to provide the needed resources.

The trick, of course, is balance.

When you create your vision statement, be aware of these four vital factors and how one must make room for the others.

Enough with the abstract. Time to get down and dirty.

Pull out a piece of paper and fold it in half and then in half again. Open it and you have four quadrants. Label these, Career, Health, Family/Friends, Community/Faith.

Now it's time to use your imagination to reveal what's lurking in that subconscious of yours.

Our goal is to distill your vision for each quadrant into one sentence followed by a brief explanation of that sentence.

Let's use health as an example.

Some do this exercise and come up with, "I want to weigh 180 lbs, be able do 100 push-ups, run a marathon, etc." This isn't vision, these are goals.

A vision might be,

"Maintain a health-conscious lifestyle that treats by body like a precious resource. I will feed my body foods that will allow me to reach peak performance, I will exercise to reduce the chances it will break down, and I will avoid pollutants that will cause it harm. I will do this so my body will not become a limitation to what I can do in life or be the reason I leave this life prematurely. I will do this not only for me, but for my family and friends whom I will be able to serve better in good health than in bad. I will do this because great health will allow me to reach

my peak effectiveness in all other aspects of my life."

Not bad.

A vision statement lays out what you want to do, an overview of how you will do it and, finally, the reason why it is important to you.

This is your strategy. Once in place, you get to dive head first into tactics.

The tactics are the annual, monthly and weekly actions you need to accomplish this vision.

This is where you get to target the weight goal, pick that marathon you want to run 10 months from now, choose the size of clothes you want to fit into, etc..

The three secrets to proper goal setting are:

1. Set big goals.

2. Immediately break them into the smallest pieces possible

3. Turn these pieces into SMART goals.

Your goals should be elephants. They should be big, audacious goals that stretch you as a person and take you out of your comfort zone.

The problem is that when you set an elephant-sized goal, you can suddenly find yourself scared to death of it.

The old question: How do you eat an elephant?

The answer: One bite at a time.

Once you set a huge goal, the first thing you do is check it against your vision. If it's consistent with your vision, then you move on to step two.

Break down your goal into steps, both in level of accomplishment and the time you give yourself to achieve the goal.

Want to run a marathon?

Find the marathon of your choice and print out something to symbolize the goal. Maybe it's the website for the race. Or simply a page from a calendar with the date circled.

Whatever it is, put it somewhere that it will be in your face. The bathroom mirror is my favorite. I brush my teeth every morning and every evening standing in front of that mirror. Instead of looking at my ugly mug, I look at visual representations of my goals. That way I start my day (what am I going to do today to forward my goals?) and end my day (did I execute my plan today?) thinking about my goals.

In our marathon example, get the best advice (a coach, if possible) on how to achieve your goal. A running group with an established marathon training program is the easiest route. If unavailable, a training schedule is a Google search away.

The easy way to hold yourself accountable is to make sure all of your goals are SMART.

Specific: Leave abstract notions for your vision statement. These goals are to the point, easily understood when described, and leave no room for interpretation. Don't get cute, set a goal that is indisputably concrete.

Measureable: Something you can't measure is easy to achieve...you can just say you accomplished it. Who's going to argue with you? This is the reason unmeasurable goals are useless. The old adage is, "What gets measured gets made." Don't say you're going to run to stay in shape, say you're going to run 10 miles a week. Don't say you're going to read more, say you're going to read a book a week. You get the point.

Attainable: Are you reaching for something that is even possible? This may seem like a no-brainer, but you would be surprised how many people I work with who aspired to goals that are simply unattainable. Can you drop 15lbs before your beach vacation...in 5 days? Can you write the great American novel in two weeks? This isn't about imposing limitations. It's about your goals meaning something...like that you can actually accomplish them!

Realistic: So you want be a movie star by your next birthday? I like the way you're thinking. But unless you can break that down for me in bite-size pieces, I'm going to throw a flag on the play and argue that you're not setting a SMART goal. It's not unrealistic that you can accomplish this goal someday, but your timeline might need some work. Break it down into a small goal, give yourself a deadline and get to work. Who knows, with the right amount of hard work and dedication, you might just pull it off. Movie stars exist because they successfully followed their dreams, right?

Timely: A goal without a deadline is a daydream. Set a specific amount of time you have to achieve your goal. Anything over a month and you need another goal underneath it to break it into smaller bites.

So, set big goals that are aligned with your vision, break them into pieces, and then be SMART about them.

But be careful what you wish for. If you follow these steps, those wishes might actually become a reality.

SECRET #2
FOLLOW THE CODE

*The reputation of a lifetime can be
destroyed with a single act.*

-Chinese Proverb

Look at you. All charged up with a great vision
statement and SMART goals to implement your
plan. Before we get too far ahead of ourselves, we
need to take a minute and take another look at that
vision statement.

Maybe you are a naturally conscientious individual
and your vision statement is filled with references
to your values and how you want to extend those
values into the world around you.

But I've been doing this long enough to know that
we probably have a little work to do in this area.

Nothing happens in a vacuum.

As you move through the world you impact those around you just as they impact you.

The breadth and depth of that impact is impossible to know, but it is my belief that the ripple effects of our transit through life are much larger than we imagine.

One of my favorite movies is Frank Capra's *It's A Wonderful Life* with Jimmy Stewart. If you've somehow managed to make it through the 100+ times it plays on TV every Christmas without seeing it, I suggest you check it out.

In this movie, Jimmy Stewart wishes he had never been born. To help save his soul, an angel shows him an alternate world where all the good he had done in his life is erased, exposing the chain reaction of events his good works had created.

I love this movie because in highlights one of the guiding beliefs in my life.

I believe our actions carry themselves deeply into the world, much farther than our immediate circle of influence would suggest.

This residual impact magnifies our opportunity to create good (and evil) in everything we do. Every decision, no matter how small it may seem at the time, can have unexpected consequences that outsize your intentions.

A small act of kindness to a stranger may change that person's mindset at a pivotal moment in their life. A derisive or rude comment can push someone further into self-defeat and cause them to turn away from their opportunity to make a positive impact on the world with their own actions. You just never know what the true consequences of your actions will be.

This is why it is so important that you live by the Code.

The Code is a series on non-negotiable values upon which you will base your actions and decisions as you move through life.

Every hard moral question becomes simple when you follow the Code.

Every decision you face becomes as easy as laying it next to the Code to see how it measures up.

So, what is this Code?

Unfortunately, I have no idea.

I know what mine is. I have a carefully defined written set of values to which I try my best to adhere. (I say try my best...I'm not claiming sainthood here.) These values are non-negotiable and provide guidance for my decision making.

My Code is something I try to live instead of preach, so I tend to keep it to myself. But I will give you one example.

Part of my Code is that I will not stand silent in the face of racism or bigotry. I believe silence is culpability.

Sometimes this part of my Code is easy to follow. Sometimes it's not. Once upon a time at a dive bar in California I found myself toe-to-toe with a big, mean biker-dude who decided he wanted to show me his "White Power" tattoo. I guess he thought we could be pals. Self-preservation told me to be quiet. The Code spoke up. I told the guy what I thought of his tattoo. ("I find your racist views completely distasteful," was the actual quote.)

Fortunately, the bouncer broke up the fight before my face hurt the guy's knuckles too badly.

So, what did the Code do for me? What impact did that little episode make on the world?

Truthfully? Who knows?

Maybe the friends I was with that night saw what I did and spoke up against bigotry some other time when it was inconvenient to do so. Maybe the hundred times I've told that story in seminars (and now to you) makes someone stand up to racism. If nothing else, my four kids will know the only time their Dad was ever in a bar fight was because a bigot tried to spread hate and their Dad's Code made him speak out against it.

That alone is worth the price of admission.

Having a Code based on non-negotiable values ensures that your vision and goals don't become fulfilled through the sacrifice of your humanity.

Can you get rich by cheating other people and taking advantage of them?

Happens every day.

You have to decide if you want to be part of that scene or not.

My business partners and I feel so strongly about values that our company has established and published its values for all to see.

We require every prospective employee to self-identify that they agree with and can adhere to these values as part of our organization.

For example, our first value is, "Relationships are everything." This value guides our daily decisions, including whether an individual is a good fit for our culture.

If someone in a leadership position is obviously sacrificing relationships to drive revenue, we make a change.

We're not socialists, it's just that we believe that a values-based organization based on a "Relationships are everything" philosophy will create a stronger company in the long-run and create more revenue in the correct manner.

Not only that, but an organization where "Relationships are everything" is a place I want to go to work every day.

A place that serves no purpose other than to just make money isn't interesting to me.

Many companies follow a Code of, "Create shareholder value," as their core value. Every decision is seen through this prism. Does X action create a result that adds to shareholder value?

This isn't wrong. It's just not my Code.

What's your Code?

What are the non-negotiable values to which you are willing to dedicate yourself?

If you're having trouble answering this question, an interesting way to approach it is to imagine the values you would hope your kids will hold.

Work it out. Spend some time on this (writing it all down, of course) and then stick it in a drawer for a week. You'll find your mind will continue to mull it over that whole week, but wait the whole time before you work on it again.

While we're waiting for that week to pass, I want to add this side note.

Sometimes people ask to see a sample of a completed Code...meaning would I share my Code with them.

There is nothing wrong with sharing your written Code with others. In fact, some would argue that if you broadcast it to the world, you are more likely to follow it.

Personally, I keep my Code to myself. I don't want it to be a self-aggrandizing manifesto about morality. (I'm also a guy who donates to charity anonymously.) It's a personal Code so I keep it that way.

I challenge myself to make my Code obvious to those around me through my actions, not by waving a piece of paper over my head.

What you do with your Code is up to you. After all, it's your Code.

OK, our week of waiting is over.

Open that drawer, pull out your Code-in-progress, set aside an hour, and work through what you have written down. You will find ideas to add, things you want to subtract. Put it back in the drawer. Come back to it to check in on how you are doing every few months...for the rest of your life.

Nothing happens in a vacuum. Make the execution of your goals in pursuit of your vision grounded in non-negotiable values.

Live by your Code and make that Code something that brings positive energy to the world.

SECRET #3

OWN YOURSELF

*A man's greatest strength develops at
the point where he overcomes his
greatest weakness.*

-Theodore Roosevelt

It is very hard to take full responsibility for your
actions and the outcomes your actions produce.

Politicians spend their entire careers successfully
dodging that bullet.

Whatever the circumstance, there is always a
convenient scapegoat that you can use to avoid
responsibility.

If you get bad grades, it's easy to blame the teacher.

If you hate your job, it's fun to complain about your
boss.

If you are unhappy, it's convenient to point to the circumstances that surround you. Circumstances that are, of course, out of your control.

It is easy to *say* we should take personal responsibility for our actions, but it is a much easier *action* to assign blame to other people.

This avoids being self-critical which can be a painful, ego-deflating process.

When we push off the blame to someone else, we conveniently avoid any unnecessary pain.

I want to show you that personal responsibility does not have to be a burden, but actually creates a strong base for achievement.

An ethic of personal responsibility forces you to take sole custody of your mistakes and failures, but ultimately allows you to own your life.

Sometimes it is hard to take responsibility because there truly are external factors that affect the events in your life.

You might be from a very impoverished neighborhood with terrible schools, or you might have some kind of physical condition that makes success in some areas harder for you than for others.

Faced with incredible obstacles, people react in different ways.

Some use it as a crutch for why they cannot be successful.

Those who pluck the most from life simply work harder for success because they refuse to let their environment and condition dictate their lives.

I have met some incredible people in my life who have decided not to bow down to circumstance.

It helps me to remember these incredible people when I face my own personal obstacles.

For example, when I struggled with my grades in school and wanted to blame my teachers, I thought of my friend who put herself through college while working a night job and being an incredible single mother.

When I get tired physically, I think of the people who come to the gym in a wheelchair and work out twice as hard as I do.

When I feel low about someone I know having success only because their parents helped them, I think of the great stories of people who have risen from incredibly humble beginnings through their dedication and hard work.

It is easy to blame others, but stories of those with greater struggles than our own can remind us that we have the power to overcome any obstacle.

Even if you have a horrible teacher, you can make yourself learn.

Some of the greatest minds in history taught themselves out of books without the benefits of a formal education. Abraham Lincoln passed the bar after studying on his own at the public library. He couldn't afford law school, but he did not allow that to stop him from his goals.

Some of the greatest leaders started as simply another face in the crowd.

To paraphrase Mark Twain, "Every person is given twenty-four hours a day. Some people just seem to accomplish more in that time than others."

Whatever odds you are up against, there is an important fact to keep in mind.

Someone before you has faced larger odds and bigger obstacles, but they made it.

They persevered and defeated the odds.

Knowing that, face down every obstacle with the knowledge that you can choose to overcome it.

It has been done before, and there is no reason why you cannot do it again.

If we can agree on this premise, then we agree that only you can be responsible for your success.

If it has been done, it can be done.

Don't sell yourself short and blame your circumstances or other people.

When you assign blame, you say that you are not as strong as the people who have beaten the odds.

If you live in a high crime neighborhood where survival is a full-time occupation, think of the people who made it out.

If you face racism and bigotry, look at the people who have overcome those obstacles.

If you have a physical handicap, look at the people who still compete in sports and lead incredible lives.

Surprisingly, when you accept complete responsibility for your life, an incredible burden is lifted.

The term 'burden of responsibility' makes it sound like you have to carry the weight of the world on your shoulders.

The weight is actually lighter than you might think.

The true weight comes whenever you blame someone or something for your failures because you are saying that the direction of your life is out of your hands, beyond your control.

What a statement!

Imagine if I came to you with this option.

I agree to relieve you of all personal responsibility for your happiness and success.

In exchange, you agree not to choose the direction in your life and to allow your limits to be dictated to you. I will be the scapegoat for all your shortcomings and in return your choices will be confined by the limits I place on you.

What a horrible existence!

But that is exactly what you say when you blame your failures on anything other than yourself or give up on a dream because of some obstacle.

We are too quick to give up on our dreams because...

"That is a male-dominated field."

"I need to know someone in the industry."

"I had terrible teachers and my GPA was too low in college."

"It would be embarrassing to try and fail."

When you buy into barriers and allow them to defeat you, you give that barrier power over you.

The crazy thing is that people choose to accept narrowed possibilities in their lives because they buy into limitations.

An obstacle that you accept and do not fight against is an excuse.

It is a way to shift responsibility away from your obligation to overcome the barrier.

Condition yourself to always accept responsibility and look at every obstacle as a test over how much control you want in your life.

To take responsibility is to take control.

When you take control, your life will never be confined by your circumstances or by the prejudices of those around you.

This happens only because you choose to make it happen.

When obstacles impede your progress, you accept the responsibility to find a way around them.

Maybe the path will be easier for someone else, someone with family connections or more natural ability.

Who cares?

You have your work to do and an obligation to yourself to persevere and realize your potential. Personal responsibility is a statement that your life is controlled by the actions of one person, you.

When you assign blame, you give power to whatever you blame.

So, be in charge of your life. Choose not to live as a reaction to the people and circumstances around you. Choose to take responsibility.

It will be one of the most powerful moments in your life when you do.

SECRET #4

TRY LIKE A BABY

It's not whether you get knocked down, it's whether you get back up.

-Vince Lombardi

Are you ready for the best advice you will ever get?

Late one night, I was driving through Arizona on my way to New Mexico and I was listening to an Anthony Robbins tape that a friend had given me.

People tend to have mixed emotions about Robbins, everything from best speaker ever to over-rated cheerleader. I find he has a straight-forward, concrete approach that provides a powerful framework for achievement.

That night, as the dark desert whipped by me on my long drive, he used an analogy that made a lot of sense.

He was talking about perseverance and the ability to bounce back from failures and he asked a simple question...

"How many times would you let a baby fail at walking before you stopped it from trying anymore?"

That got me thinking and by the time I reached New Mexico, I had this chapter written in my head and what I think is the best advice in the world.

Approach every difficult goal that you set for yourself like a baby learning to walk.

If you have ever watched a baby trying to take his first steps, it looks painful.

It's a lot of falling down, crying, bruises, wobbly legs and frustration.

If you watch the early attempts, it seems impossible that the baby will ever walk.

So, as Anthony Robbins asked that night, how many attempts to walk would you give a baby before you stopped him from trying?

How many failures would it take before you decided that a perfectly healthy baby would never walk?

How many times would he need to fall down until you decided that he should just crawl for the rest of his life?

You can look at a baby and know that no matter how many tries it takes, he will eventually learn to walk.

It makes perfect sense when we talk about a baby, but what about when it comes to your life?

How many times are you willing to fail at your goals before you give up?

If you started with the assumption that eventually you would make it, would you ever give up?

If you give up too soon, are you willing to go through life as a "crawler"?

Think about that for a second.

Imagine that you were fully developed intellectually when you tried to learn to walk.

After failing to walk a thousand times, you allow your frustration to overcome you and you decide that you will never be able to walk.

You stop trying.

You can see that other people are able to walk and that they had just as much trouble as you, but "they're just lucky," because they made it.

Imagine your life as a 'crawler.'

Think of the limitations you will have placed on yourself and experiences that you will have thrown away.

A 'crawler' will never run a race, hike through the mountains, or jump in excitement. By giving up on a difficult goal, your life experience will have been irrevocably diminished.

Each time you fail at something you have the power to decide whether you call the failure a defeat or another step toward success.

Think of the dreams and goals you want to achieve and imagine that there are two possible worlds.

One where you achieve your dreams, and one where you lower your expectations to meet 'reality.' Basically, imagine one world where you crawl, and one where you run.

Do you feel the tragedy inherent in even the possibility that some choose to crawl?

To have the ability for greatness, but to stop short simply because of frustration?

All you need is the concrete belief that you will reach your goal. You will walk eventually. It's just a matter of when.

A few more 'baby' points:

- **Success follows success.** After a few days of wobbly steps, confidence grows and you try to walk more often. With enough practice, you can literally walk in your sleep. If you want to be brilliant at something, do it over and over again. The best professional athletes are those who practice and train the most.

- **Success allows greater success.** As confidence grows, a simple walk becomes a run, a dance, or a jump. Be great at whatever you do because this gives you the confidence to stretch yourself in new ways and create more success.

- **Rewards encourage success.** A baby walks to get something. She walks to her parents, walks to food, or walks to satisfy a curiosity. What reward drives you? Make the reward so strong that you are driven to your success.

- **Learn from people who have experience.** It helps when you are a baby to be surrounded by people who already know how to walk. Surround yourself by people who are successful in their lives for these same reasons.

One of my favorite music lyrics is by Seal. *"In a world full of people, only some want to fly...isn't that crazy?"* That one sentence encapsulates this entire chapter.

Choose to run. Choose to fly. Not to do so would just be crazy.

SECRET # 5

GET LUCKY

It's hard to detect good luck – it looks so much like something you've earned.

-Fred Clark

One of my hobbies is to collect information from very successful people to determine what made them a success.

I use autobiographies, second-hand accounts, and personal interviews to try and get down to the elemental ingredients for success.

One of my favorite conversations was with my own grandfather, a retired two-star General and World War II veteran.

General Joseph May had a successful military career and rose through the ranks by placing first or second in every officer training class he attended.

He spent his career also trying to learn how successful men designed their lives and carried themselves.

His exposure to successful individuals was broader than my own as he was able to speak with major military leaders, governors, and several U.S. Presidents.

I sat down with him as I entered my pre-life crisis in my early 20s and asked him for advice.

I wanted to know what made success.

What were the secrets he had learned through those years of development and exposure to major personalities?

He was quiet for a while, eyes squinting slightly as he formulated his answer.

I waited for what I knew would be life-changing advice.

"Every person I know who was truly successful..." he started, "all possessed the same fundamental quality."

Now I'm dying. What is this one quality? What is the secret?

"Every person who is successful is that way because they are extremely lucky."

Lucky!

This is the great advice I get to steer me on my future!

What a rip-off!

"But," he continued, "you have to define luck in a very specific way. Luck is when opportunity meets preparation."

Luck = Opportunity + Preparation

Now, General Joe wasn't the first to make this point. (This quote has been attributed as far back as Seneca, the Roman philosopher in mid-1st century AD.) But coming from my grandpa, I paid close attention to what it really meant.

If we look at this as a mathematical equation, there are two constants and one variable.

Luck, which can also be termed 'the result' or "success', is a constant because we determine how it is defined.

Everyone perceives success in different ways.

If you get a big promotion at work, one of your friends might congratulate you, while the other sympathizes with you because you will now have more responsibility and less free time.

Opportunity is also a constant.

I often get an argument on this point because there is privilege in the world and not all opportunity is equal.

However, I have met people from an extremely privileged background who have done nothing with their lives, and I have met people who have risen from abject poverty to accomplish amazing tasks.

Is it more difficult to rise from poverty than to slide into the family business?

Absolutely.

But opportunity exists, and it can be captured. While the ease of capturing opportunity varies, the existence of those who overcame great personal odds to rise to high office or station clearly demonstrates opportunity exists for all.

That leaves only one variable, preparation.

People can define success, and opportunity exists for everyone, but preparation is usually where the equation breaks down.

What are you willing to do so that you can take advantage of opportunity and create the luck you want?

For example, I interview people all the time who want to go into international business.

This is an exciting and high growth field with incredible opportunity.

I ask them what languages they are willing to learn to be a success in this field.

Nine times out of ten, the candidate says they do not like languages and are going to work with English speaking countries.

Obviously, someone who is not willing to prepare for a career in international business by learning a language will not be very "lucky" when the time comes to enter the job market.

Preparation never stops because:

1. **You can always improve.** The greatest athletes always practice the most. They are the first on the field and work hard to always improve.

2. **Opportunity is unpredictable.** You never know when new options will present themselves. The key is to be prepared to take advantage of any opportunity that serves as a vehicle for your skills. Suppose you meet someone who owns their own business and they need a new director of sales and they

have to hire someone right away. If you have created a strong background built on concrete results, you just got "lucky."

Pursue luck/success through preparation. If the preparation is difficult then you have to gauge the level of commitment to your goals.

You have to decide internally how serious you really are about your goals. Don't waffle. Don't equivocate.

Don't blubber that what you're trying to accomplish is too hard, takes too long, or that life is unfair.

Either buy into your goals 100%...or change them.

That last comment might surprise you, but it's important to understand that it is OK to change your goals.

The trick to changing your goals is to make certain you are changing them for the right reasons.

If you are changing because your initial goals are "too hard," "require more what than I thought," "are too unrealistic," or anything in this vein, then you are selling yourself short.

If you are going to make a big change on direction, make certain it is direction only, and not reach.

What do I mean by "reach?"

To me, goals are like Olympic diving. You get extra points for difficulty level. I'm all in favor of setting short-term goals that are very reachable to give yourself some quick wins and boost your confidence. But your overall goals need to reflect the intrinsic ability with which you were born to accomplish something worthwhile in the world.

The reach of your goals measures their difficulty level and whether they are truly an aggressive attempt to fulfill your potential.

Change your goals if you wake up one morning and find that you have put your ladder to success against the wrong wall, but don't trade out the extension ladder for a three foot tall stepping stool. Maintain your reach and you will never lose your personal path toward what you were meant to achieve.

SECRET #6

GO INTO CLONING

*The person who says it cannot be done should
not interrupt the person doing it.*

-Chinese Proverb

Learn from people who have what you want.

Success requires an incredible amount of painful
trial and error, but there is no need to re-invent the
proverbial wheel.

The trick is to learn as much as you can from other people's errors so as to avoid the pain yourself.

Clone the positive character traits you can learn
from successful people and use them to create your
own success.

The term "secret of success" implies there is some magical formula out there that will ensure your happiness.

Unfortunately, there are no cure-all formulas, but there are some lessons learned from experience that can help you to speed through the learning curve.

Success and happiness seem like elusive goals, but people do achieve them and these people have the 'secrets' you need.

If you want to be wealthy, find wealthy people and find out what makes them tick.

If you want to be a better communicator, find someone who impresses you and pick their brain for a while.

Successful people are eager to help others (and usually eager to talk about themselves.)

It really is as simple as asking, "How did you do that?"

Most people have to fail over ten times at something before they figure it out.

Each failure gives them new insight and instincts to prevent the next failure. It is a gradual process of constant re-adjustment and re-thinking.

The exciting thing about role models is that you have a guide who has done the homework for you.

They can guide you through the land-mines and tell you war stories about the mistakes they made early in their careers.

One warning about role models.

Listen carefully to the advice you receive and be aware that not all of it will be useful. This can occur in any interview and often in the case when there is a significant generation gap.

I had a female friend who wanted to go into international business so she found someone prominent in the field and met him for lunch to learn about his career.

The conversation was full of advice and war stories from fifty years of business experience, but his general point was that women should not go into business because they would not be respected!

This concept is obviously outdated and was more than a little insulting to my friend (who, by the way, is now a highly respected businesswoman.)

Take advice from anyone and everyone you meet, but keep a clear head and use the advice that makes sense to you.

In my friend's case, she took a lot away from that conversation that helped her career. Also, she used the man's attitude about women in business to prepare herself for other people she would meet in her career with the same attitude.

Use any advice that will help you get to your goal, but filter the advice with your values and your level of ambition.

For example, if you want to be an executive in the film industry, a conversation with an old industry veteran will give you incredible insights and advice.

But, if you are impatient for success, you also want to find the person who achieved success at a young age and find out how they did it.

Find a role model that most closely resembles your circumstance and who has what you want.

Obviously, there are certain skills and lessons you have to learn on your own. There is no substitute for experience to learn intangible skills like leadership, good communication, empathy, and tenacity.

Also, there is always advice you will not believe and sometimes you have to just find things out for yourself.

However, a good role model can show you the best way to gain those skills in as short a time as possible.

There is misconception that this advice is limited to college students researching career choices. Not so.

This is an effective strategy no matter your age and no matter the skill you want to acquire.

Think of the novelist or screenwriter developing a story about police. Anyone worth their salt will arrange ride-alongs with the police in the same setting as their story to live and feel the world they are describing.

If you are in your 30s or 40s and considering a career change, find and interview a dozen people in that field.

Use role models in every part of your life. In your career, your personal life, everything.

Be a dedicated life-learner and find the best teachers.

You have a limited amount of time to reach your destination and a good guide always helps make a journey easier.

SECRET #7

BE UNCOMFORTABLE

To get what you've never had, you have to do what you've never done.

-Eleanor Roosevelt

It is human nature to acclimate to environment.

We adapt quickly to change, but we prefer the status quo because it is comfortable and known.

People love to complain about their circumstances, their job, their boss, but they seldom do much to change.

Regardless of how much you like or dislike something, the fact that you are used to it places it in your comfort zone.

The comfort zone includes everything that you are used to, anything that you can do without thinking twice about it, anything that you know you can count on.

A comfort zone can be a good thing.

Your family and friends are part of your comfort zone. Possibly your religious faith is in your comfort zone.

These are the things that give us a foundation and support throughout our lives.

However, sometimes too much comfort can derail your goals for your future.

There is inherent stress whenever you try something new.

Stress comes from the unknown and change usually involves the unknown. Therefore change tends to bring stress while the status quo, even if it is not what you want, is comfortable.

For example, have you ever stayed in a relationship longer than you knew you should?

Most people have at some point in their lives.

They are not happy with the person they are with, but the unknown of being alone or trying to find someone else keeps them in the relationship.

You will have to face very difficult choices throughout your life.

When these decisions come up, it is always easiest to choose the path that is most comfortable, it will be the decision that produces the least stress and uncertainty.

But, do you think that staying in your comfort zone will lead you to the achievement you want?

The challenge is to be conscious of your comfort zone and actively pursue challenges in spite of it.

It is difficult to do. If you maintain the status quo in your life, you will not have stress, you won't be nervous about tackling something new, you will have less fear of failure.

However, accomplishment begins with attempt.

If you never attempt the things you fear, they will hold you and your ambition captive.

Complacency due to comfort will slow you down and allow your aspirations to move farther and farther away.

Choose action over comfort and challenge yourself to do what you fear.

It's the only way to truly find out what you can accomplish.

SECRET #8
GET SOME PAIN

It's a very short trip.   While alive, live.

-Malcolm Forbes

There is a theory of human behavior that all actions are a reflection of two basic motivations:

1. Avoid pain
2. Acquire pleasure

Every action can be traced back to one of these motivations.

For example, you will take a sip of coffee because you anticipate the pleasure of the taste and warmth of the drink.

If the coffee is too hot and you burn your tongue, you will not take another sip of coffee until it cools off.

You want to avoid the pain so you wait until it can offer pleasure.

This is not a new concept. Motivational speakers have created entire philosophies and self-help programs based on this simple premise.

The reason so many motivation gurus have jumped onto this concept is because it actually works. It taps into a deep part of the human psyche that responds instinctively. If you can learn to control these instincts that are hard-wired into your brain, you can accomplish nearly anything.

The tricky part is to identify sources of pain and pleasure and how we associate these with different parts of our life.

If you are over-weight, you have a constant battle between pain and pleasure.

Food represents immediate pleasure and gratification, while being over-weight may create pain if you feel unhealthy or unhappy with your appearance.

As a rule, the battle between pain and pleasure goes to whichever is more immediate.

Pleasure is not as exciting if you know you have to go through pain to get there, and pain does not seem as bad if we get some pleasure first.

Negative consequences are never on our minds when we are having fun and experiencing pleasure. If they are, they are often a fleeting thing.

"Ohhhh...I really shouldn't have that piece of cake. Well, if you insist."

When we allow our actions to be dictated by the most immediate consequence, it is an instinctual reaction.

Our instincts demand that we pursue pleasure and avoid pain.

The best way to create positive changes in your life and maintain your commitment to your goals is to change how you associate pain and pleasure with your actions.

This pleasure/pain paradigm can explain most behavior. For example, let's talk about whether you did the exercises at the beginning of this book. (If you did, you're off the hook.) If you did not, let's figure out why. Was it the discomfort (pain) of self-reflection? The annoyance (pain) of spending time writing instead of doing something you really wanted to do.

Whatever the case, you were not convinced that the exercises would give you enough pleasure to make the effort (pain) worthwhile.

Now, imagine that you knew with 100% certainly that the exercises in this book would make an enormous positive influence on your life.

Imagine that there was no doubt that they would help you define your future, prepare for it, and ultimately capture it.

What pleasure you would feel if you could achieve your dreams and your goals?

Imagine the tangible results, money, a nice house, recognition from your peers, satisfaction, whatever you covet.

Now, take the tangible feeling of that pleasure and place it on top of the pain that the exercises might cause you.

Doesn't the pain pale in comparison?

Next, take the mental image of your future success and throw it out the window.

Imagine yourself unable to achieve your goals, stuck in an unrewarding job that you hate, unable to quit because you are in debt.

How does this result make you feel?

What pain do you associate with this outcome?

How will you feel if none of your ambitions come true, even though you had the opportunities to make them happen?

That is some very serious pain.

That is the challenge.

You have to pick whatever your hot button issues are that you know will make you act.

You can convince yourself that the short-term pain is worth it for two reasons. First, the pleasure will be worth it and second, there is a greater pain for not doing the activity than the pain for doing the activity.

Working out to get in shape is a great example.

If you are out of shape, exercise is the last thing in the world you want to do.

When you exercise you are forced to recognize how out of shape you really are. If you do not work out, wear baggy clothes, and avoid mirrors when you are naked, you never have to admit it.

The short-term pain of exercise is enough to make most of us avoid working out altogether. But if we associate the pleasure of being in shape and the pain of being unhealthy with the act of exercise, it is easier to get into the gym.

To really do some fool-proof association, you have to make it concrete and make it personal.

For the working out example, your associated pleasure might be a trip to the tropics in two months and the pleasure of wearing a new bathing suit, or the pain of being embarrassed to wear a bathing suit if you do not work out.

Maybe the association is to run a race for charity and the pleasure you would feel by helping your community, or the pain of not running the race after you told your family and friends about it.

Choose whatever hot-button issue will motivate you to get into the gym. If it doesn't work, you have to find a more powerful association.

The challenge is to associate the possibility of future pain with the behavior you a trying to modify.

If you want to make yourself do the hard work required to research and determine the right career path for yourself, then associate that activity with your level of commitment to your future.

If you want to get in shape, then associate the activity with the pleasure of a future event.

If you can't get up in the morning and the pleasure of sleeping-in is too tempting to pass up, train yourself to immediately think of the consequences to your behavior.

I am the original hate-the-morning, hit-snooze-a-thousand-times, late-riser.

I mean, I used to hate to get up.

But, when I do manage to get up early, I love the quiet of the morning and I feel good about my accomplishments.

One day I decided to wake up every day at 5am to get a jump on the day and capture the pleasure I felt from being up early.

The first few mornings were horrible, but I became used to it after a while and now I am a habitual early-riser.

I used pain association to break my sleeping habit.

I convinced myself that sleeping in made me accomplish less and made it less likely that I would achieve my goals.

If I couldn't even demonstrate the determination to get out of bed, how could I succeed at my life goals?

Sleeping in now symbolizes to me a lack of determination and will and I am not willing to accept that I do not possess those traits.

Even today, I have an internal dialogue as I sit on the edge of my bed every morning after I have turned off my alarm.

All of the great reasons why I should lay back down and sleep come flooding to me.

My best argument to myself is that if I lay back down, how dare I assume to teach others how to achieve their goals?

Case closed.

Up and off to the shower I go.

(For the record, I'm not advocating sleep deprivation! I may be early to rise, but I'm also early to bed. Studies show proper sleep increases mental acuity. Get your eight hours – just figure out when the most impactful hours of your day fall and show up for them.)

Add pain to your life by associating it with behavior you want to change.

Also, be aware that short-term pain sometimes is necessary to avoid the long-term pain of unfulfilled ambition.

For example, suppose you want to quit smoking.

Obviously, there is short-term pain when you quit because of withdrawals from nicotine, but also because you lose pleasure.

But what if you fully felt the long term pain your habit will cause you?

This works with any habit that you want to change.

Try it.

Write down the ambitions you have for your life and then describe how you would feel if you were actually able to accomplish them.

Now, use the same list and describe in detail the pain you would experience if you were unable to make it happen.

Using the smoking example, imagine a day spent with your future grand-children and develop the pain if you die before you can have that experience.

Imagine your spouse as he/she ages alone and uncared for and ask yourself if inflicting this pain is worth the pleasure of a cigarette.

Associate the behavior with the pain.

Every time you pick up a cigarette, force yourself to think of the different levels of pain that cigarette will cause.

What character failure do you demonstrate if you are unable to control your behavior?

Why is your short-term pleasure more important than the pain you will cause the people around you?

Next, associate pleasure with your behavior change.

In the example above, cigarettes become the pain of loss and abandoning your family, but the action of not smoking represents a decision to have pleasure in your life.

It is an empowering feeling.

You are creating an action or behavior to give yourself long-term pleasure and fulfillment.

The short-term pain can be difficult, but once you connect the behavior change with your future pleasure, you can start to welcome the pain because it brings you a step closer to fulfillment and pleasure.

Every day of pain when you stop smoking is a day closer to losing the craving.

Every morning of pain to wake up early puts you one step closer to achieving your goals.

If you acknowledge the source of your motivations, it is easier to control your behavior.

Ultimately, when you add pain and pleasure through association, you are more likely to successfully create the behaviors you expect from yourself.

The decision is yours.

SECRET #9

PRACTICE VIVID LIVING

The unexamined life is not worth living.

-Socrates

Life is short and far too important to spend casually.

Take advantage of the great opportunity you have to capture all of the adventure that life presents.

On one side, we are creatures of habit. We fall into a routine and stay there until something forces a change.

When we go somewhere new, we say, "give me a few days to get into the swing of things," which is code for, "let me find a monotonous routine so I can feel comfortable."

On the other hand, we are escapists who dream about adventure and excitement.

We go to the movies and watch television to see people live the lives we want.

We see exotic locations, live incredible romances, and go on wild adventures.

All this while we lounge on the couch with a bag of chips and a soda.

Imagine if you used just one half of your 'escape time' to ensure that you lived an exciting life, instead of watching one.

Again, life is short, and in the end, all we have are our experiences and the impact we made on the people around us.

Of course, there is the daily grind, laundry, walking the dog, washing dishes, but this is no reason to force yourself into a continual grind.

The next time you choose to watch TV or sleep in instead of living vividly, use this question to test yourself.

Five years from now, will I remember this day?

What a powerful question!

If you do not remember the day, and no one around you does either, what purpose did it serve?

I'm not saying that you have to spend every day fighting crime or working for a cure for cancer, but live to create memories that you will remember.

A day of hanging out with friends or family can be a memorable day, if you make it so. Every day doesn't have to be an earth-shattering adventure, but we are all prone to having the routines of life steal whole blocks of time away from us if we are not vigilant.

When you're lying on your death bed, I doubt you will be thinking back on all the great TV you watched over your life.

Find the things in life that drive your imagination, stretch your limits, and create a positive influence on your environment.

Create as many memories for yourself that you will actually remember.

Live life with intensity, with full vividness.

There is a great bumper sticker that says,

'Turn off TV. Turn on life."

Escape into a better life for yourself instead of into the lives of others.

If you do it right, if you actively seek out opportunities to create once-in-a-lifetime experiences, you will find they start to present themselves more often.

Often, it's not a matter of finding the opportunity, but just taking the opportunity when it is there.

A simple example.

I was in Cancun on a business trip. We took buses to the Mayan ruins of Chichen Itze and stopped at a cenote on the way there. Cenotes are these amazing sinkholes that dot the Yucatan Peninsula that often expose an underground water supply.

This particular cenote was enormous, like a massive underground dome with the roof lopped off. The water was several hundred feet deep. Jungle vines crept up the walls. A shaft of light shone down from the opening and blazed on the water.

It looked like we were in an Indiana Jones movie.

Although this was once a sacred watering place, it is now open for swimming to the strong of heart. You can hike down a path to a lower ledge and jump in. Pretty cool.

I walked up to some of the people in my group standing on the edge.

There was no-one swimming.

No-one had brought their swimming suits.

So I said to them,

"Twenty years from now, you are either going to remember swimming in a sacred Mayan cenote in the cool waters from deep inside the Earth, surrounded by a cathedral of rock and bathed in a beam of light."

I paused for effect.

"Or, you're going to remember that you had a chance to do that and skipped it because you didn't want to get your shorts wet."

Five minutes later, we were all in the water.

And it was awesome.

 A truly vivid experience.

Seek out opportunities...then take them.

SECRET #10

FOOL-PROOF STRESS REDUCTION

*If you want to test your memory, try to
remember what you were worrying
about one year ago today.*

-E. Joseph Cossman

Stress has become a fixture in modern life.

Many of us have come to view stress like it's just
part of our bodies. Something we have no choice
but to carry around with us.

Others view stress as excess baggage, something
you can choose to put down and leave behind.
Leave the bags, take a carry-on instead. Or maybe
just a toothbrush and an extra pair of underwear.

Which world-view you subscribe to is up to you.

Either way, the starting point to control the stress in your life is to understand its source.

This is the easy part because most stress comes only from one source – the unknown.

If you absolutely know something for a fact, you rarely stress about it.

Your boss calls you in for an unscheduled meeting – stress.

Someone tells you the meeting is about a promotion – no stress.

Someone tells you the meeting is about your poor performance – stress, not due to the meeting but because of the uncertainty of the results the meeting will have.

I know people who will stress for days because they have a big unknown.

They get a speeding ticket and agonize for days whether they are going to lose their license or not.

They work through every possible scenario of how their life will change if they lose their license.

Finally, after days of stress, they call the courthouse and find that their license is fine.

No more stress, but what a waste of energy!

Another manifestation of the unknown is stress from "too many things going on."

Sometimes the world seems too crazy to handle and everything is spiraling out of control.

Small issues can become enormous when they are pushed into such a cluttered background.

You find yourself with an overwhelming feeling of stress, but you find it hard to put your finger on an issue that could cause it.

Here are a few tactics you can use for stress control. I challenge you to actually do the exercise right now in the space provided. Why wait? I promise you it's worth it.

Fool-Proof Stress Reduction Exercise

1. **Write down what is stressing you.** Have you ever told someone your 'big' problem and halfway through the story you started to feel petty because the problem sounded dumb? Things we stress about often are dumb, but they get built up in our minds to be bigger than they actually are. Write down your problems in as simple language as possible. You may find yourself laughing at them.

2. **Write down a proposed solution to what is stressing you.** It's amazing when

you complete this step how simple some of the solutions really are.

If you are stressed about an "unknown" out there, how can you turn that in to a known?

Stressed about how your boss views your performance? Why not just ask her? Stressed about money (or lack of it?), what are potential solutions? Cost cutting? A second job?

Write it down.

3. **Analyze the costs of your solution.**
   Most problems come down to a solution of time, money or a little of each.

   Finding out "unknowns" take time (and sometimes a little guts). Making up a cash shortfall costs time in a second job.

You get the point. Write it down. Be as specific as possible.

4. **Get help implementing your solution.** Don't carry the weight of the world on your shoulders.

   There are plenty of people willing to help out. Parents, friends, career counselors. If you're stuck on what a solution might be, ask around. Trust me, advice is something most people find easy to give.

   (Taking good advice doesn't come as easily. For example, are you actually doing this exercise or just reading it? See what I mean?)

5. **Put your problems into perspective.** Think of the most stressful week you had in a past job or in school. Pretty bad, right? Now imagine something truly

important happened during that week – your parent was diagnosed with a major illness, a sibling was in a car accident, whatever. Do you think that any of the things you stressed about in school or in work would have even entered your mind if you were faced with a true crisis?

Below, rate the things you are stressed about on a 1-10 scale, 1 being you're not sure where to take a date on Friday, 10 being you just found out a loved one has cancer. Makes a difference, doesn't it?

Great stress management truly comes down to keeping things in perspective and jumping into problem-solving mode instead of worry-mode.

I'm not telling you to be apathetic and not care when small things go badly, but don't let the small things paralyze you and keep you from enjoying life.

Our time is way too short to lose sleep because someone gave us a dirty look or because we put a dent in the car.

Big deal.

A year from now you will not even be able to remember most of what you are stressed about today.

Don't believe me?

In the space below, write down in detail what you were so stressed out about a year ago.

There might be some big concerns (how to afford school, choosing a career, etc.), but the little stuff is long gone, right?

Stress will always be part of your life. It's a sign that you care about what happens to yourself and those around you.

But it is easy to allow these concerns to fester in our minds and allow them to poison our outlook on all of the good in our lives.

One small issue blown out of proportion can impact everything you do. I mean, don't you find it hard to appreciate a sunset when you are mad at the world?

Use stress to wake up your instincts for action and apply yourself to solve problems and uncover the unknown. Trust me, you'll enjoy more sunsets.

SECRET #11
THE IMPORTANCE OF OPTIMISM

In the long run, the pessimist may be proved to be right, but the optimist has a better time on the trip.

-Daniel Reardon

A central theme throughout this book is control.

Control over decisions, control over actions, and control over eventual outcomes.

We are all responsible for the life we create for ourselves and for what we give back to the world around us as we move through it.

We face choices every day and our reaction to these choices determine the impact our passage through time creates.

Our minds allow us to be instantly creative or destructive, positive or negative, wonderful or terrible.

You walk down a sidewalk and you see a homeless person begging for money.

- As you pass by, you dig into your pockets and give him the change you find there.

- As you pass by, you laugh at him and shove him off the road.

- As you pass by, you stop to talk and convince him to find help at a shelter nearby and promise to stop by tomorrow to see how he's doing.

- As you pass by, you look at him across the street because you crossed over to avoid the encounter.

These scenarios show the best and worst of us.

We are all capable of each reaction and each is a decision about how we view and interact with the world.

I remember a conversation from many years ago with a friend of mine.

It's one of those strange, unlikely memories that insist on staying with me, improbably surviving through the years when more important events should have replaced it.

My friend Sharon was the classic over-achiever type, valedictorian, athlete, and so on, who attended Pepperdine University while I was at University of California at Santa Barbara.

It was during a late night car ride between these schools that the conversation turned philosophical.

Sharon was talking about how she couldn't do everything she did without a strong religious background to act as her support system.

She couldn't understand how I, who was not very religious at the time, could sustain myself without the comfort of a faith structure.

I replied that my support was a faith in the basic goodness of people, the idea that people want to improve, they want to help, and they want to make the world better.

She could barely contain herself, "Oh my God, you are so naïve," was her not-too-subtle reply.

She went on to describe her own view of people, her voice and body language betraying the hurt behind her words, "People are back-stabbers, willing to step over you to reach their own goals, eager to see you fall so that they can stand taller.

They are purely self-motivated and you have to be the same way just to stay even with them."

Maybe this conversation stays with me because I remember feeling so profoundly sad for her.

As she described her views all I saw was the cage holding in the potential she had to appreciate the best in people and to share in the finest aspect of our humanity.

It's the old saying...

"Your prejudices will not disappoint you." Look for the worse in people and you will find it. Or look for the best in people and you will find that instead.

There is a fundamental truth in that.

We can find whatever we look for in people's behavior. That being the case, why not look for the best?

Why not expect and perceive the best intentions in behavior?

Why not assume people are good and start there?

Why not give people the benefit of the doubt?

Why not be prejudiced for people instead of being prejudiced against them?

Optimism does not have to be naïve.

It is not being Voltaire's Pangloss and looking through rose-colored glasses, writing every disaster off as a great adventure.

Optimism can simply be giving each person and situation the benefit of the doubt.

For example, picture yourself stuck in traffic on the freeway. You're late for an important meeting and the stress is giving you a headache. You see in your side mirror that there's a car driving fast on the shoulder, skipping by all the traffic while you sit there. Anger swells up in you. "Who does this guy think he is?"

So, you yank on your steering wheel and edge onto the shoulder just enough to block his path. The car stops, horn honking, lights flashing. You pull out a little farther and block him even more. A window rolls down and you roll down your own, ready for a fight. Instead, the man in the car shouts, "My wife is about to have a baby. I'm trying to get her to the hospital as fast as I can. Will you move?"

Suddenly, the action that you found so outrageous seems completely reasonable. In fact, you probably will try to think of other ways you could help.

My challenge to you is why not start off assuming people are doing things for the right reasons until something proves otherwise?

Optimism is confidence in your ability to impact any situation to create a positive result. It is a demanding hobby, finding the best in people, but it can fill you with energy.

Doing the opposite can drag you downward, sap your strength of purpose, and tear away at your capacities. Negativity breeds negativity.

Decide what prejudice you will use to view the world.

You will find that the more you look for good, the more you will find, both in others and in yourself.

SECRET #12

DIE A LITTLE

Live each day like it's your last, 'cause one day you gonna be right.

-Ray Charles

You've made it. Eleven secrets that, should you decide implement them, will dramatically change your ability to accomplish your dreams.

Each one a mix of practical advice and philosophical notions of how your world-view impacts your actions and how those actions cast ripples far beyond your imagination.

But I promised twelve secrets, not eleven.

The truth is, there is no limit to the number of "secrets" I could have included in this book. Life is the greatest of all mysteries and how to live it well is the subject matter for generations of authors that came before me and for the many generations who are sure to follow.

None of us have the market on the real secret to a successful life. All we can do is use the culmination of our experiences to discern what we feel are the most applicable attitudes and actions to describe this abstract notion of "success."

What has been interesting to me is that many of these chapters were written by a much younger man than I. The first draft I wrote for several of the secrets was created back in 1998/1999 while I was still in my 20s.

I look back now with a certain amount of incredulousness that I thought my brief life had qualified me to opine about the nature and meaning of life. (I'm sure my older readers and reviewers will still have that same thought today.)

Yet, what struck me most reading these drafts ten years later was what I was able to learn from my younger, less jaded, more optimistic self.

Perhaps it is the destiny of every generation that their sharp edges (and opinions) become worn by the rumble and tumble of the act of living. As I re-read the musings of my 20-something year old version of myself, I felt a re-stirring of the idealism found mostly in the young.

We can achieve whatever we set our minds to accomplish.

Life is too short to not live with intensity.

Success in two or three of the vital life factors is not enough. We must find achievement and balance in career, health, family/friends and community/faith.

I realized that even though I was living what I preached, it had become a watered down version of my own philosophy.

This led me to the twelfth and final secret.

In order to live, we must to constantly be willing to die.

Let me use writing as an analogy. By the time you read these words, I will have gone through this text ten to fifteen times to check for errors, proper grammar, coherency, etc. I know that once I lock down the draft and this book goes to print, any changes I want to make are beyond my reach.

Any typos or omissions I might find after the fact become regrets as opposed to things I can fix.

If I knew that the first draft was going to be not only the first, but the only version of the book, my writing style would have to change dramatically.

My process is to work at a manic pace, music blaring in my ears, the ideas spilling out onto the page. This may surprise you, but not all of it is that great. In fact, I assure you, it pretty much stinks.

The old saying is that writing is rewriting. Like so much excess marble in an original block of stone from which a sculptor frees a statue with his chisel, I spend a lot of time hunting for a gem or two within my reams of awful prose. The result isn't exactly Steinbeck or Hemmingway, but it's passable.

In life, there are no rewrites.

You get one draft. One chance to get it right.

And, at any time, that great big Editor in the Sky just might decide your manuscript is due.

The errors and omissions (oh, those tragic omissions) become locked. They become the regrets of a lifetime.

Just as my writing style would change if I had one draft without revisions, our actions would change if we truly embodied the belief that we must be prepared to die every day.

The key phrase here is "truly embody." Anyone can buy a t-shirt that says, "Carpe Diem" or chat over beers about living every day like it's your last.

Bumper sticker, "carpe diem" philosophy is like the Sunday preacher who prays for rain but then thinks nothing of leaving his house without an umbrella.

If you want a taste what "truly embody" feels like, do the exercise below.

Let's assume that once you finish this book (with a satisfying smile on your face, I'm sure) you suffer a massive heart attack. You've had an undiagnosed heart defect for a while now and the pure excitement from reading this book was just too much to bear.

As you float above your body, a warm light beckons you to heaven/paradise/nirvana. Remembering all those ghost movies you loved when you were a kid, you turn away from the light and decide to hang out on Earth for a while.

You decide it would be pretty cool to attend your own funeral. So you float over to your memorial service to check it out.

At your funeral:

1. Who is there? Actually write the names down.

2. What would these people say about your character?

3. What would your family say about your commitment to them?

4. What would people list as your strongest character traits and accomplishments?

5. Complete this sentence for the person eulogizing you. "The person we honor today had an incredible impact on…"

6. Complete this sentence, "The person we honor today lived life to its fullest. This is evident because…"

7. As you linger and listen to the speakers eulogize, what are the things you miss the most about being alive? What are your greatest regrets?

8. If you had ten extra minutes with five people at your funeral, who would they be and how would you spend that time? What would you tell them?

9. If you had the opportunity to come back for one day, how would you spend it? (I'm guessing you wouldn't spend it being a bad mood over a parking ticket you received or any other similar minutiae.)

What you will find within these answers are opportunities to do some rewriting now that you have time.

Haven't told your parents what they really mean to you beyond a quick, "Love ya," at the end of phone calls? Live as if you were going to die and tell them how you feel.

Have the great American novel burning a hole in your chest? Live as if you were going to die and get that book on paper.

Realize the eulogy at your funeral would not include a lot of material about how you contributed to your community or sacrificed for others? Live as if you were going to die and find a volunteer organization today.

The essential advice here is that you need to revisit this exercise throughout your life. This is why I shared with you how reading my notes from when I was in my 20s re-opened my eyes to the philosophies in this book.

In most ways, our life experiences add insight into the truths around us. Yet, the churn of adult life can also remove the vitality and urgency of youthful idealism.

If you are prepared to die every day, you can recapture that vitality and push it back into every aspect of your life. I can't ensure you will live any longer, but I believe you will have lived better.

The following is an excerpt from WAKE UP CALL, part of The Career Series by Jeff Gunhus. This and other books by Jeff Gunhus can be found at:

www.thecareerseries.com

WAKE UP CALL #1 - The world has changed. It's tough now and it's going to get worse.

Your timing could have been better.

Before you got here, times were pretty good.

First there was the technology boom where it seemed anyone with a day trading account and a dart board could make a quick fortune.

During that same time, fresh-faced college grads found themselves lured to start-up companies with stock options that often turned into big paydays, sometimes worth millions.

Traditional employers battled back and developed perks and comp plans and vacation policies to compete for Gen X and Gen Y talent.

Then real estate was the new thing. Everyone got "zero down" loans and flipped houses.

Money flowed.

Life was easy.

Then, in a blink of an eye, it was all gone.

Bummer, huh?

The world financial markets collapsed, real estate values plummeted and behemoths like GM declared bankruptcy.

Employers everywhere woke up and had the same resounding thought, "Workers need me more than I need them."

And, my dear job-seeker, that new ground truth for employers is not good news for you.

A few headlines:

COLLEGE GRADUATES TACKLE DISMAL JOB MARKET
– CBS News

COLLEGE GRADS FACE TOUGHEST MARKET IN YEARS
– ABC News

COLLEGE DEGREE NO SHIELD AS MORE JOBS ARE SLASHED – Washington Post

Some stats from the 2009 National Association Of Colleges and Employers (NACE) *Student Survey*.

- Jobless rate for college graduates DOUBLED with over 2 million college graduates unemployed.

- Employers will hire 22% fewer college graduates this year.

- Only 19.7% of graduating seniors who actively sought jobs in 2009 landed one before graduation.

- 40% of graduating seniors believe they will find a job but will still need financial help from their parents.

- CNN reports 80% of 2009 college graduates moved back in with their parents.

- As of July, 2009 the economy shed over 7,000,000 jobs!

And the really bad news?

The economy has gotten much worse since these surveys were taken!

And don't fool yourself that you can hide in grad school until this blows over (or that you can stretch out your undergrad a couple more years).

The changes happening in the economy are systemic and long-lasting.

Things will improve eventually, but even when they do, the job market will be tough for a long time and never return to the easy days of multiple job offers at firms eager to entice you with creative perks. Which leads me to my next point...

WAKE UP CALL #2 – The negative impact of graduating into a bad economy will last for the first 10-15 years of your career.

I have to admit, this one even surprised me.

I thought it reasonable to assume that once the economy got back on its feet, recent college grads who had taken low-paying jobs to get by after graduation would just slide back into great career trajectories and get back on track.

Unfortunately for you, this is not the case.

A recent study by Yale economist Lisa Kahn found that college students who graduate in recessions experience a significant decrease in compensation for the first 10+ years of their careers.

When will the good news end, right?

Ms. Kahn's research attempted to understand why the phenomenon occurred. While it's impossible to assign the entire effect to one cause, she does put forward a likely explanation.

Evidence shows that college grads that enter the job market in a recession are forced to take jobs of a lesser stature than college grads graduating in normal or good economic times.

New entrants into the job market slave away at these "make-do" jobs for a couple of years, waiting out the recession.

Once the economic good times get back in full swing, they apply for, and often get, better jobs.

However, the skills developed at the lower paid "make-do" jobs rarely transfer into a useful skill in the new position, so the job seeker has to basically start all over.

For example, say a finance major graduates in 2010. No one in the finance world is hiring (and if they are, they can hire one of the thousands of laid-off finance gurus with **significant prior experience**), so the finance major gets a job with AT&T as a store manager.

Two years (and hundreds of cell phone upgrades later), the financial markets are hopping again and there are job openings at the investment banking firm that was once the finance major's dream job.

First, our poor finance major might not even apply. Once in the job market for 6 months or more, individuals become sedentary and resistant to change.

Ever wonder why you see people with "10 Year Anniversary" badges checking your groceries at the supermarket?

Second, our finance major is a little out of touch with her finance background. She hasn't exactly been practicing derivative pricing models or modeling bond market fluctuations on her lunch breaks.

Even with her "work experience" she might be a less attractive candidate than someone about to graduate who just crammed for their final in Advanced Financial Market Strategies.

Third, if she does get hired, our finance major will be essentially starting from square one next to recent grads 2-3 years younger than she.

What is really disappointing is that the statistics show that even in cases where the job candidate gets into their career 2-3 years after graduation, it will still take over 10 years for that grad to "catch-up" to where they should have been.

Unfair, isn't it?

The real question is, what are you going to do about it?

Complaining about the state of the economy is like complaining about the weather...it ain't gonna change anything.

All of the data shows that the negative effects of graduating during a recession come from taking a less-than-ideal job after graduation.

The solution?

You and I need to make sure you are one of the few who get a great job after graduation.

Even in a terrible economy, there are success stories and there are great jobs to be had. To get one, you will need to not only execute a flawless job search, but take the steps to turn yourself into an irresistible candidate.

This book will show you step-by-step how to do these things and not only get a job, but get started on a great career. All you need to do is put in the time and the hard work.

If you don't, it could take you 10-15 years to recover from the mistake.

WAKE UP CALL What Every Young Adult Must Know To Survive Today's Job Market

ISBN 1-4486-5507-2

$16.95 (paperback)
$14.95 (ebook)

Are you ready to face the toughest job market in a generation? Can you compete with the thousands of unemployed workers with significant prior experience willing to take an entry-level position? WAKE UP CALL not only explains what's happening in the job market, but teaches you how to be one of the lucky few who get a great job after graduation. (Only 19.3% of 2009 graduates had a job at the time of their graduation!)

If investing a couple of hours will give you an edge to get the job you want, why wouldn't you do it? You owe it to yourself. It's time to WAKE UP, smell the recession and get to work.

GET YOUR COPY AND ACCESS FREE CAREER ADVICE AT

www.thecareerseries.com

HOW TO CHOOSE THE RIGHT CAREER...You So Don't Waste Your Life In A Job You Can't Stand.

ISBN 1-4486-7959-1

$16.95 (paperback)
$14.95 (ebook)

You're going to spend half your waking hours either at work or thinking about work. Isn't it worthwhile to make sure you're choosing the right career? ***How To Choose The Right Career*** *takes away the guesswork and shows you how to confidently make the right decision.*

With simple to use exercises and techniques, you will be able to finally figure out exactly what you want for a career. Even if you think you know what you want to do, shouldn't you make sure you're headed in the right direction before you begin the journey?

GET YOUR COPY AND ACCESS FREE CAREER ADVICE AT

www.thecareerseries.com

www.ingramcontent.com/pod-product-compliance
Lightning Source LLC
Chambersburg PA
CBHW051532170526
45165CB00002B/699

*   9   7   8   1   4   4   8   6   8   1   3   7   2   *